A Long Weekend on the Sofa

Kenny Knight

A Long Weekend on the Sofa

Shearsman Books

First published in the United Kingdom in 2016 by
Shearsman Books
50 Westons Hill Drive
Emersons Green
BRISTOL
BS16 7DF

Shearsman Books Ltd Registered Office
30–31 St. James Place, Mangotsfield, Bristol BS16 9JB
(this address not for correspondence)

www.shearsman.com

ISBN 978-1-84861-501-4

ACKNOWLEDGEMENTS
Thanks to the editors of the following magazines where some
of these poems previously appeared: *The Broadsheet, Epizootics, Litter, The Long
Poem Magazine, Plymouth Herald, Saw, Shearsman, Tears in the Fence.*
'The Van Dike Club' originally appeared online in
A Festschrift for Tony Frazer.

Many thanks to my Private Secretary (unpaid), Sara Elizabeth Smiles,
for viewing the manuscript prior to publication.

Contents

For
Tim Allen,
Norman Jope
and
Steve Spence

Chatsworth Gardens

It's been another quiet day
on the street and night
has fallen for itself again.
The sun has torn itself
into billions of pieces
and has gone back indoors
and is shining through the windows
at a speed quicker than anything
driven by Henry Ford.

I'm sitting on the front doorstep
looking out over my mum's privet hedge
at the houses on the other side of the street
the street where we live
with cats and dogs and goldfish.

When I open the letterbox
I am blinded by brightness.
I can see my sisters
wandering from room to room
as if they were on the beach
slowly getting suntanned.
I can hear the wireless
and the second hand clock
ticking in the background.
I can hear my mother
talking to herself
and talking to the cat
and talking to the ghost
sleeping in the shadows
of the wall.

If I looked around the corner
I would see my father

sitting in his deckchair
on Treasure Island
a monosyllabic parrot
sunbathing on his shoulder.

Like a jackdaw flying home
across the St. Budeaux Triangle
I wish I had somewhere to go.
A walk down to Shakey Bridge
to see the trains and wobble
like a big dish of jelly.
A night out with Queen Log
and Grand-daughter Grizzly
a picnic on Honicknowle Green
or a neighbour's lawn
or just someone to call around
to see if I'm coming
out to play outer spaceships
in the dark.

I was eating my tea
when my friends
wandered off
gone into the fog
that fell so thick and suddenly.

Are they walking
in circles around
the Honicknowle Theme Park?
Are they sitting on the wall
behind Harpers Garage
or leaning
on each other's shoulders
outside the fish and chip shop?
leaving me here
gazing at streetlights

watching moths
head-butt council property.

I walk part way around
the outside of the house
and open the back door
quietly follow my shadow
into the promise of sunrise
as another day on the street
turns on its heel and toddles off
leaving me here like a poem
all by itself in a big notebook.

Treeline

The family tree
is one tree

in the forest.
The family tree

is wild and long
and in need

of a haircut.
On the branches

of the family tree
my great grandfather

and his crew
of pirates

and jackdaws
were shipwrecked

in the desert island
resort of Las Vegas.

The one-armed bandits
and roulette wheels

made them homesick
for the seaside.

My great grandfather
was six foot seven.

Not very tall for a tree
out in all weathers.

For a bit of peace
and quiet he'd sit

on the family tree stump
or climb into the crow's nest

to read the autobiographies
of the dead.

My great grandfather
had a pirate ship

a fleet and a flock
of jackdaw flags in every port.

My great grandmother
planted sons and daughters

in the birthday parties
of the future.

The family tree
is root and driftwood.

On my father's side
a monkey puzzle

on my mother's
a silver birch.

A Christmas Card on the Wind

The jackdaw
wants to hotwire
the Elizabeth the Third
and go around the world
just to get away
from the Royal Wedding.

From the washing line
the jackdaw takes a flag
and a party dress
and irons out the creases.

On one side of the flag
there are two robins
sitting on the shoulders
of Robin Hood.

One day this flag
will fly over the rooftops
of sheds, shops and houses.
A flag in a world without thrones.
A flag for my hometown.

On one side of the flag
there are two robins
leaning on a garden fork
happily married or happily not.

Two robins flapping on a string.
A Christmas card on the wind.

A Short History of Children

My father was born
in Nineteen Twelve
the same year as Roy Fuller,
Woody Guthrie and Lightnin' Hopkins.
It was the year the Titanic went down.

In the village of Hatherleigh
my mother's eyes popped open
it was Nineteen Fifteen
and the news was dark
the First World War
hadn't yet stuck a bayonet
into a birthday cake
it was barely nine months old
and crawling all over Europe.

Over in America Muddy Waters,
Brownie McGhee and Billie Holiday
were starting out on the road
to amplification.
Back home my mother
picked up her teddy bear
and moved to the outskirts
of town and into
the Nineteen Twenties
the era of slapstick.

In Nineteen Thirty Three
Chatto and Windus published
the collected works of Wilfred Owen.
My father read about life in the trenches
while my mother went to the cinema
and marvelled at the waste of custard.

By thirty nine
the golden age of quiet
had long gone and soundtracks
filled the rooms of Hollywood House.

By Nineteen Forty Two
there were bombsites
all over the city.

Married in forty six
Monica arrived in forty seven
It was a year rich with future
post-war celebrities
Pam Ayres, Iggy Pop,
Mitch Mitchell and Warren Zevon.
George Orwell was weeks away
from starting Nineteen Eighty Four.
That year in baby boom town
it was Ry Cooder's first Christmas.

Brand new like Nils Lofgren,
Jaco Pastorius and Jonathan Richman
I followed four years later
narrowly missing Halloween.

In Nineteen Fifty Six
Angie Wickenden was born
in Hatfield to a daughter of Tipperary.
It was a leap year the year
Walter de la Mare, A. A. Milne
and Jackson Pollock died.

Twelve months after
Winnie the Pooh went into mourning
I was in Class One at West Park Infants
trying to get to grips
with the English language.

It was Nineteen Fifty Seven
the year Somerset House
signed Sid Vicious
and Susan started playing drums
in the family band
two years before
Christina was born
in Hanover on Christmas Day.

Trout Fishing on Treasure Island

The jackdaw landed
on the newspaper boy's shoulder
and impressed us with its knowledge
of pirate history.

When I asked, on how many seas
had it flown the flag of the jackdaw
it blinked seven times
and plucked a telescope
from the newspaper boy's pocket.

The jackdaw had just
flown in from Hollywood
on a day as dark
as Alfred Hitchcock.
It was the size of a baby raven
and more coherent than a cat.
It was hopping from one foot
to another on a stage
of cotton and bone.
It was a moment of wild magic
on the road to the village
of Weston Mill.

When the jackdaw parted company
with the newspaper boy's shoulder
it looked back over its left wing
as the treasure hunters
unrolled the map it was flying across.

By the time
we reached the village
rain had started to fall
so we found shelter

and a pile of damp letters
in a terrace of derelict houses.
It was hard to tell which parts
of the correspondence were grief
and which parts the consequence
of inclement weather.

Moving from house to house
I imagine the families
of long forgotten Plymothians
roosting in quiet corners.
The Grim Reaper
had been and gone
quicker than the rain.
We discovered this when we went
searching for the jackdaw's money
and found nothing inside a bag
of grass clippings.

If we could locate the jackdaw's house
we might uncover its accumulated wealth,
but would it know fool's gold from sixpence?

On the day the jackdaw was born
the rain fell and grew everything.
The land, as wild as a cabbage
and blokes with long beards
flooded the market.

After learning to fly paper cormorants
from the roof of the old aquarium
the jackdaw circumnavigated
Tinside Pool and Plymouth Sound
explored Devil's Point and Drake's Island
and stopped for lunch
on top of Smeaton's Tower
where it stuck a telescope

through the eye socket of a skeleton
so the dead could see the stars.

Weaned on narratives of adventure
the jackdaw sat in the crow's nest
reading books by Richard and Robert
as the Elizabeth the Third
sailed off for a spot
of *Trout Fishing on Treasure Island*.

On its first day as a seadog
the jackdaw wore blue dungarees
to match the colour
of its aquamarine plimsolls.
It cleaned its dungarees
every afternoon after lunch
with its mum's vacuum cleaner.
The vacuum cleaner
had a very long lead
and was useful for navigation.

On a black sea horse
the jackdaw went show jumping
across the seven hurdles of the ocean
and spent many long hours
collecting for its pension plan.
It bought a villa in Spain.
A chalet on Whitsand Bay
and deposited money
in various high-street banks
in Reykjavik.

With the pound weakening
against the dollar
and inflation rising
like the sun on a cold morning
the jackdaw opened the curtains

and its last bottle of rum
before heading for the horizon
and the free market
while drunkenly contemplating
the vagaries of boom and bust.

The jackdaw
is a stranger to seasickness
and brand new to paying taxes.
A pirate long before the long ship
a geologist of dubious credential
who spent part of its career
being monitored by CCTV
and the other half
by nuclear submarines
from Devonport and the USSR.

The jackdaw is a social creature
huddled together in derelict bliss
huddled together like a city of houses
at home in churches and cathedrals
until the dove fell from grace and rapture
and the jackdaw moved
from the House of God
to the ghost town end
of the property market.
At night it dreams
of Fleetwood Mac's
Albatross
flying solo
above an acre of woodland.

Every morning as regular
as the tide it starts the day
with a cough from the past.
It's got one slipper on
and one slipper off

and it's ready to go.
It's got a memory
like a foggy day in West Park.

Like Edward Lear's seafaring owl
it found a niche through the pen
of Ingoldsby
in the fabric of nonsense verse.
It was rocking and rolling
out on the surf long before
creationists crawled out
of the primordial swamp
and discovered
how to shoot moose.
My mother tells me this
when I return from the village
of Weston Mill
slipping this news
into my gloved palm
like a baton passed
from one generation to the next.

Herzog's Window

The grass
has given them a home
they share it with horses
and bad tempered rhinos.
They come here
to paint antelopes
and big woolly mammoths.

There must have been
crows and ravens and jackdaws
and the sky would have been as noisy
as a pub crawl, but there are no birds
on the walls of the cave.

Tonight in the dark cinema
I'm a prehistoric groupie on sabbatical
from the gold mines of the future.

The landscape around the Ardèche
reminds me of the Honicknowle Hills.

I'm a big tall poet
writing on the walls of cyberspace,
but I'd rather be a cave sniffer
like the Master Perfumer
in Herzog's film.

I'd like to shake
the hand of the man
with the crooked finger
and hear him play
Star Spangled Banner
on a prehistoric flute
as he dances under darkness

with Palaeolithic bison
in the galleries of the past.

If I could smuggle
myself back to the Ardèche
I'd gather bunches of wildflowers
to brighten the darkness,
plant prehistoric garden gnomes
in the caves at Chauvet
just like the ones my dad found
on the allotment in Nineteen Sixty Three.

Beneath the floors of the grass
we come to paint the first coat of magic.
In the cinema the light shines
on our faces from Herzog's window.

We make movies
and I daydream in the dark
on Angie's shoulder.

We walk with wolves
and paintbrushes
and read the palm
of the man
with the crooked finger.

The land has given us a home.
We share it with crocodiles
and big tall horses.

Scarecrow

Before the allotment was an allotment
blackbirds sang and the scarecrow slept
in the breath of the forest.
Before history occupied
the bookshelves of the future
and the squares of our cities
the scarecrow waded out of the sky
wrapped itself in a beach towel
and stuck bits of driftwood
to its slender frame to give it mobility.

Moving with the blues,
greens and golds
under the radar of the trees
and the dark hills of the sky
the scarecrow wandered off
to find fame and fortune
on the front pages of newspapers
and a niche in nothingness.

Now the gate opens
and a shadow moves
across the allotment.
There are treasures
that lie beneath the soil
the roots of spring and piracy.

On induction day in the allotment
the scarecrow scares a flock of sparrows
and dreams of promotion.
The next day it follows a wheelbarrow
through a jungle of mixed fruit and vegetables
and thinks about becoming a store detective
scaring shoplifters in the local supermarket.

The wheelbarrow reminds the scarecrow
of the wheelbarrow in that poem
by William Carlos Williams.
It's heading for the compost heap
and a career in poetry.

On the Duke of Cornwall's birthday
it enters a poetry competition
where the first prize
is a packet of polo mints
awarded by the lead vocalist
of the Buckingham Shed Collective.

One day a robin lands
on the shoulder of the scarecrow's
bright Salvation Army uniform
the previous owner
presumably gone to Box Hill,
Efford, Weston Mill or Ford Park.

The scarecrow is indigenous,
but on quiet days it nods off
to somewhere postcards aren't sent.

When it rains the rain brings out
the scarecrow's sadness.
Hat, coat and trousers
dripping like a clothesline.
The scarecrow's shadow, however,
stays as dry as the shadow
that hangs around with Nietzsche.

The landscape of piracy
is the landscape of the allotment.
Pirates come here to swashbuckle
with bees
and jackdaws pluck bright feathers
from the scarecrow's good nature.

One afternoon after reading
Trout Fishing in America
the scarecrow walks across the allotment
flapping its arms like a farmyard chicken.
Guided by Abercrombie's post-war pencil
it adds an East Wing and a West Wing
hangs portraits of store detectives
in the Museum of Scarecrows
as October turns to November
it supervises the renovation
of Buckingham Shed
reassembling it to resemble a ship.

At the end of each working day
it goes home to its wife
and scarecrow children
takes off its hat and coat
and gazes at the stars
beyond the beauty
of the paraffin stove.

Plimsolls

After lunch I walked
all the way from Honicknowle
to meet you.
Stretching myself
on the map of the day
long legs on long leafy streets
a working-class adventure
to the posh part of the city.
I tied my plimsolls
in a double knot.
It was a nice kind warm day
that greeted my departure
and shared my arrival.

It was Sunday and children were out
sunning themselves in back gardens,
jumping over black holes
in the cracks of pavements.
It was the lollypop lady's day off
so like a boy
hurrying to the sweet shop
I crossed the road carefully.

There was a map of the city
in my shirt pocket
and a piece of string
for nothing in particular.

Fifty years after Scott
left home for the Antarctic
I set out to explore
the ice cream streets
of my hometown
with a packet
of Fox's Glacier Mints

and a bottle of tap water
to sustain me
through this wilderness
of suburbia and birdsong.

Reaching the summit of Box Hill
I sat on the wall of the graveyard
to read my collected teenage poems
and for an encore
a little whisper of Edward Lear
to the shades of sleeping Victorians.

On the day we met
I was a pilgrim
to the patron saint of plimsolls
repeating the number
of your house
over and over again
so that when I got to paradise
I wouldn't get lost in Mannamead.

That day you were destined
to become the first poet
to read my collected teenage poems
and in retrospect
the honour to be the last.

You were the Queen
of a poetry circle
not much bigger
than the parish
of a rain puddle
the bus splashes through
on the way into town.

When you were my age
did you go searching for poetry
maybe stand in the wartime crowd

at Mount Wise
when Louis Aragon
stepped ashore after sailing
from the land of surrealism.

After walking from Chatsworth Gardens
I was ready to write my memoirs.
Hot and sleepy
I fell into a Mannamead future
a long way from home
and the Honicknowle Dream.

When your husband
opened the door to your house
on Compton Avenue
he reminded me
of someone
from *The Munsters*.

I remember nothing specific
about our conversation.
I know we talked about poetry
lifting the lid a little
on haiku and free verse,
but the details of that meeting
are as distant as the shadows
that stretch across the seconds.

I can only now vaguely recall
the dim faces
from the Plymouth Writers' Club
the once-teenagers
out of the Nineteen Forties
writing poetry in dark shelters
of the ground.

Drugged up to my eyeballs on adolescence
and down to my plimsolls on chewing gum

I was a teenager from another part of town
a paper boy made of wood made of words
a hundred different stories
written on the sheets of my skin.

Before we met
I thought all the poets
were collected together
in graveyards
and now a dozen years
after your passing
I'm curious to know
what became of all those
unpublished sonnets
and villanelles
you left scattered
tidily around the house.
Maybe hidden behind
the ventilation grille
waiting to be discovered
like the mermaids
in Emily Dickinson's basement —

or gone like my collected teenage poems
and my plimsolls to the posh part of the city
gone like you to take your place
with Wallace Arnold and Wallace Stevens
gone to tap a cultured foot
on the Persian rug to Mahler or Haydn
gone for a tea break like the string quartet
to discuss Eliot, Frost and Ziolkowski
with Doreen and Gabrielle and all those other
middle class lollypop ladies with lollypop concerns.
There are no lollypop ladies
in *The Honicknowle Book of the Dead*
though there might be a sweet wrapper
or two folded between the pages.

Reading Rosemary Tonks

For Tim Allen

I'm in Waterstone's again
hanging out in the poetry section
with Tim Allen
he's at the top of the alphabet
in the company of Pam Ayres
and Elisabeth Bletsoe.
I'm a little further down the stack
a few spines either side
of Miroslav Holub and Frank O'Hara.
The years lie collected between us
all the way from Aragon and Bashō
to the younger generation
of Jope and Spence.

Upstairs in Waterstone's
we find our books leaning
in a long sleepy line
dreaming of Honicknowle
and Portland.

Fifty quid lighter
we head down Gandy Street
with books by Harry Guest,
Peter Redgrove
and Christopher Middleton.

Driving fifty miles
from my hometown
across the country
to the old city of Exeter.
Hanging out with *The Voice Thrower*
dropping words all over the pavement
kicking the English language

along the street
two left-wingers
dribbling down the architecture
towards five minutes of fame
collected together
under a dark spotlight.

In the hustle
and bustle of the Phoenix
Tim heads for the Box Office
while I toddle off to the bar
to hang out with John Hall,
Philip Kuhn and Lee Harwood.

Over in the poetry section
a man dressed for motorbike travel
takes a copy of *Chocolate Che*
off the shelf
and drives across
the island of Thursday night
towards another Black Box reading.
Upstairs that night at Uncut Poets
Tim opens for Damian Furniss
while I open for Kelvin Corcoran
with *Three Quarters of a Ten Bob Note*
my homage to homelessness
and Rosemary Tonks.

For All the Communists in China

For Angie Wickenden

The day is a ripple in a diary
the sun rises and slurps over
the rim of my cup
spills golden drops of itself
into the saucer.

I drink tea whatever the weather
or the politics that condones
the spilling of blood.
I'll never stop drinking tea.
I wouldn't go into rehabilitation
for all the communists in China.

I don't take sugar and I don't make mugs,
but if I was a cubist I might open a café
on St. Budeaux Square and call it Picasso's.

My body is a shrine to the teabag.
My religion is a mouthful
of hot pleasure.

I drink a cup of Camellia Sinensis
on the anniversary
of writing *Lessons in Teamaking*
and drive fifty miles with Angie Wickenden
to buy two bags of clay
from a small industrial estate
on the outskirts of a sleepy village.

We pass through Woodbury Salterton
like mice through a cat flap.
The hedges and verges are trimmed
to barbershop perfection.

The wealth is understated.
The village pub is called the Digger's Rest.
The name conjures up a sense
of archaeology in waiting.
It's the kind of place
where if you snored at night
you'd get an ASBO.

On the way home
I fall asleep and dream
of a cafe under willow trees.
I'm reading the daily horoscope
and stargazing the compatibility
of a brown-eyed Piscean
on Old Town Street.
I reach for the milk
across the constellation
of the *Western Morning News*
and clumsily spill tea over dreams
grown plump from fiction
and my interpretation
of that is to sleepwalk
down to the corner shop
and buy a map of Honicknowle
and a dozen boxes of Darjeeling.

A lifetime of astrological minutes later
and I'm back in the canteen at work
sat next to the corridor which leads
to the warehouse and the supermarket.
I'm having lunch with myself again.
It's been a long journey
from the State Cinema
to a State Pension
from William Cookworthy
to Angie Wickenden
and *Lessons in Teamaking*.

Tea has changed
the colour of my eyes
making them a deeper blue.
Tea is perfect to start the day
as you are perfect to start the day
the afternoon and the evening
and after dinner I'll meet you
at the Bagatelle for a cup
of Camellia Sinensis.

A Short History of the Mini Skirt

On the High Street I shop for history
drop the swinging sixties into a carrier bag
eleven mini-skirts for eleven girlfriends.
Picking up my packages
I head downtown to Old Town Street
to drink a cup of coffee at the Bagatelle.
Under the willow trees,
under my new haircut
I flick through Fleet Street photographs
of Jean Shrimpton and Mary Quant
and read a short history of the mini-skirt
which doesn't take very long.

Further up the street
on the edge of the new arcade
the children of Rupert pass through
the doors of the teddy-bear shop.
Around the corner
generations of family trees
wait for buses on both sides of Royal Parade,
carry designer bags home to the suburbs
of Badgers Wood and Holly Park.

As I drink the last of my coffee
I take a tarot pack from my shoe
and shuffle myself a hand
which points in the direction
of the sundial.

These days I never leave home
without reading the *I Ching*
or consulting
The Book of Random Access.

Leaving the Bagatelle
I follow the crowd
onto New George Street
and down beyond the sundial
seek refuge in the bookshop.

I push through the doors
and become another coffee drinker
under surveillance, another face
in a star-studded cast of cut-ups
auditioning for CCTV
and *Crimewatch*.

I walk the aisles inside the bookshop
looking for Jack Kerouac and Jack Reacher.
From there I cross swords with sorcery
remember *Mort* with fondness
and Neville the part-time barman
remember just in time to swerve
around Vic in top hat and plimsolls
swashbuckling time-travellers
from some long forgotten Wednesday.
Browsing trilogies of Science Fiction
I imagine being abducted by aliens.
Unzipping my rucksack I clutch
The Book of Random Access
as if it were a getaway car
or a short cut to an episode of *Star Trek*.

When the time-travellers stop for a tea break
I follow them up the stairs to the poetry section
where I find my homage to childhood
loitering between books
by Norman Jope and Philip Larkin.
Over-optimistically I think
The Honicknowle Book of the Dead
should be more popular

than books about the end of the world
or rain dancing in a temperate climate
and really should be a bestseller
like Dan Brown's *The Da Vinci Code*
and maybe should have been called
The Honicknowle Diaries of Nostradamus.

Trying to look inconspicuous
I hang around town until the late afternoon
reading poetry and scanning the body language
of pedestrians until growing tired of gravity
and the crowd and the nightlife
creeping into town like the tide
under the bridge at Laira.

On Royal Parade
I catch a number twelve bus
and chat to the driver
who looks slightly pagan
with stone circle eyes
and that old solstice rigmarole.
On the Viaduct
a blind man climbs on board
waving a white stick
like a magic wand
and for a moment
the bus is suspended
between Outer Mongolia
and the road to Crownhill.

After Mutley Plain it all gets residential
we climb the social ladder to Mannamead
and a minute after passing the outskirts
of Manadon
turn down the road to Woodland Fort.

When I get home West Park is quiet.
It must be teatime or *Top of the Pops*.
Maybe everyone's fallen asleep
or have superglued themselves
to screens and sofas
watching the long mini-skirted legs
of Miss World.
When the mini-skirt first appeared
on the Crownhill Road and walked
into Easterbrooks in Nineteen Sixty Seven
it was the start of the sexual revolution
and the golden age of the hen party

When the mini-skirt
made its big-screen debut in Chelsea
it was shortly after
a little bit of nuclear war
had been let out of the cage
and onto the catwalk on Bikini Atoll

When the next General Election comes
I'll consider voting for one of the two women
I passed tonight dressed as chickens
outside the fish and chip shop
on the corner of Hirmandale Road

Closing the door on the world
I put Bob Dylan on in one room
and a tin of soup in another
and feel curiously like a feather
drifting from thing to thing.

That Day in the Park

The telegraph chatters
and I step inside
Edmund Hillary's boots
and climb the totem pole
of many voices.
Forty feet above the ground
forty years old, son from a street
of forty houses and daughters
playing blues for my father
blues for my mother
playing cross country guitar
live on air
to a crow
in conversation with itself.

The sun comes out
and brightens the day
with a far reaching glance.
Across the country
it's Mother's Day,
but not for this orphan.

The sea is older than a fairy tale
The family tree is driftwood.
My father has gone
to where my mother is
and I'm four years tall again
on top of his shoulders
a prelude to being six foot two
that day in the park.

Pirates of the Mud

The clock cost sixpence
it is twenty past seven
in Nineteen Fifty Nine.
My body is seven years old.
It makes a lot of noise.
The world is old enough
to be my mother.
My mother has a clock
ticking in every room.
She likes the sound they make.
She doesn't like silence.

When I was in the first year
at primary school
There were a family of robins
nesting in the dashboard
of my mum's Hillman Minx.
One night a shooting star
flew over the house
and my mother followed it
to Kathmandu
climbing the Himalayas
in second gear
until the car conked out
with altitude sickness
at which point
she sold that old Hillman Minx
for a Penny Farthing
and cycled back with the robins
tucked up in the saddlebags.

When I was a small boy
the farthing was the smallest coin
in the British Isles

with a street value
of a quarter of a penny.
On the back of the farthing
is a wren flying at six miles an hour.
Like wrens, robins are a part
of the indigenous
wildlife of this island.
I have always associated
robins with winter.
In the Art College canteen
they are considered models
of the English Countryside.

I recall plump bodies on thin legs
gripping the handles of garden forks
beady eyes scanning the overturned garden.
Pirates of the mud
adopted by Christmas romantics
they hang in the rooms of the house
on galleries of string.

Abercrombie Lane

For Norman Jope

I'm anonymous in a world
that's seriously tabloid
and I like it that way.
I'm fed up with living
in the rush hour heart of nothing.
I want to move to a quieter locale
a village with a green,
a row of shops, some cottages,
a Palmerston fort or two
with turrets and dungeons
and a moat for mallards,
some creeks and woodlands
with migrant birds and shelter
and a railway bridge
for jumping into the river
when the weather's hot.
When I get there
I plan to start a campaign
to reopen the footpath
across Shakey Bridge.
I want it to shake, rattle
and rock and roll again.

I'll write a proposal
to close the Parkway
and reseed Manadon Woods
prepare for the second coming
of the prefabs
and Anderson shelters on Tamar Way,
prepare for the resurrection of friendship
lost in the long years of growing up
while there's still some childhood left
and later when I'm nine or ten

go walking through an island of countryside
to the village of Weston Mill
before Broomball Lane is sliced like bread
to make way for by-pass traffic.

I'll reacquaint myself with memories
lost like all those brain cells to drugs
read the map on the back of my hand.
Set out to explore the back streets
and the back pages of the literary quarter
discuss Swinburne on Cobbitt Road
and cross swords with the shadow
of an old friend cycling to Crownhill
to audition for the part of Oliver Twist
while another searches for a soup kitchen
on Dickens Road.

On the outskirts of Tennyson Gardens
I recall my first fumblings in English Literature
where the poems written in exercise books
cringe from the light.
The future negated with no sense
of the long years yet to come
blank as a ghost wearing a sheet of A4.
A Long Weekend on the Sofa
still fifty years from completion.

On Abercrombie Lane
I'll scribble the first drafts
of *A Short History of the Mini-Skirt*
and *Three Quarters of a Ten Bob Note*.
I'll go digging for the roots of suburbia
and play cricket and spaghetti westerns
on the slopes of Wild West Park
play psychedelic blues
play free form jazz
play urban twang lemonade afternoons

with Donald's Metaphysical Greenhouse
play rock and roll garage bands
on the bonnet of my dad's car
gate-crash girl next door weddings
all over next door neighbourhood lawns
play the top ten and the Top Twenty
in a state of horizontal bliss
and get gigs in the nightclubs of sleep
drumming for Punk Yoga.

I'll be a nostalgic newspaper boy
dropping in from the here and now
with a memory detector,
a pirate's piggy bank
and an old street map
I'll be an archaeologist
coming home to daydream and take notes
coming home to trowel the lane
coming home to rediscover the past
to explore old rooms of architecture
to see the bright fires
and the bright lights burning
in the bright houses on the other side
of the muddy park.

That night I'll dream
the dreams of a fourteen-year-old
shape shift back into my old pyjamas
and in the morning when the rooster
on the breast pocket of my uniform crows
I'll crack an egg and unravel
the science of string theory
follow it to school with fifty years
of unmarked homework in my satchel.
I'll stick gold stars on brown leather
for writing essays on flying saucers,
black holes, the life forms of Mars

and the St. Budeaux Triangle
and award myself silver stars
for first drafts of *Some Imaginary Bands*
and *Playing Chess in Chatsworth Gardens*.
I'll be one of the teenage Grand Masters
of Honicknowle and West Park
taking to the streets of the neighbourhood,
moving from Kings Road to the concrete pitch
of secondary school
where I'll see fog rising from packets
of Woodbine and Park Drive
see cancer in the air on Smokers Corner
see children playing football or conkers
faces from school photographs
taken fifty years ago.

After the school register has called
two dozen names from the past
I'll tiptoe under the red lights
along the corridors of old power.
Slipping into the trousers of an old minute
I'll stand with my classmates
in the back row of school assembly
think about gold stars and silver stars
and little green men
playing conkers on the playground
think about teenagers
travelling home first class
through the Honicknowle rain
think about doormats and prayer mats
and nostalgically recall the deputy head
telling me my eyes weren't closed in prayer
and she only knew mine weren't closed
because hers weren't closed either
and I'd sit there
and stand there and endure
the harsh hypocritical light from above

then saunter off down the corridor
to the chalk pits of academia
to study with pickaxe and pen
in the classrooms of the working class.

By the end of Friday afternoon
the past will be back in my blood
and I'll be fifty calendars away
from the genetically modified future
and my second home in the palace of rats.
By Saturday morning I'll be reading
the *Morning Star* and Karl Marx
and laughing at Harpo.
I'll be washing my hands and face
and looking in the bathroom mirror.
I won't be Santa Claus anymore.
I'll be eating a plate of happiness for breakfast
and by the afternoon I'll be playing guitar
and harmonica like Big Joe Williams.
By the weekend
I'll be writing and singing the blues
after bumping into Dame Joan Vickers
at a Higher St. Budeaux summer fayre.
Hair as blue as frostbite
and politics cold enough
to freeze a socialist
into spontaneous hypothermia.
I'll be in the audience
around the back of the Blue Monkey
as she's interviewed by Dave Purvis
the political correspondent of West Park.

I'll walk from street corner to street corner.
I'll be a cat lover in a catalogue
I'll be a model of modern post-war art.
I'll walk into and under
the trees in Woodland Wood

with a map to somewhere else.
I'll walk down Milford Lane
to the railway station at Tamerton Foliot
I'll be an apprentice hobo riding the rails
and a hitch-hiker in a Steppenwolf song.
I'll fall asleep in the arms of Radio Luxembourg.
I'll fall asleep in the arms of the Shangri-Las.

Moving will be like going on holiday
back to the archaeological lands of childhood
back to the mythological lands of the dead
barefoot on the beaches of nostalgia
with a bucket and pen.

Short-Listed for Piracy

For Steve Spence

The scarecrow takes flying lessons
from a highly qualified jackdaw
goes joyriding in suburbia
gets a gold star
for navigating Box Hill cemetery
crosses a dozen bus routes
and is spotted
window shopping
window boxes and greenhouses
and narrowly avoids
a head-on collision
with a red bus in West Park
and makes it safely back to the allotment
which is as busy as a supermarket.

After lunch the scarecrow
and the jackdaw fly across town
to an old Victorian park on Paradise Road.
Gate-crashing the air-space
of a crowd of poetry listeners.
The scarecrow heckles
at the speed of tin
and passes under the radar
of cabbage whites and red admirals
just as a man dressed as a pirate
swings a disembodied microphone
around in swashbuckling style.

The scarecrow lands
on the pirate's shoulder
and gets typecast even though
its plumage is quite obviously
not a bird's.

It's the pirate's
first poetry reading
and the scarecrow's last chance
to be a stunt man
in a Steve Spence poem.

Homesick for the landscape
of Hans and Lottie
the pirate goes deep sea diving
off Smeaton's Tower
until the tide goes out
to where the stars shine.
Is it the moon doing this
or a plumber washing the dishes?
Born to fly shipments of gold
the scarecrow walks the stem
of the sunflower like a pirate.

The scarecrow takes the bus
on a field trip to London
and the pirate takes the train
after being short-listed for piracy.
The scarecrow runs into the pirate
at the Chelsea Flower Show,
but gets homesick for honeysuckle
and tea and toast
at the Crownhill Garden Centre.

The pirate is building a desert island
in the piracy of his own home.
He sings the score of *South Pacific*
in a voice that reminds
the scarecrow of George Melly.

After listening to the pirate read
But it looks like a bird cage
built by a surrealist.

The scarecrow and the jackdaw
follow a passing cormorant
over to Drakes Island,
but don't know the names
of any pirates who live there.

Curious about shipwrecks
and the archaeology of desert islands
the pirate swaps his swashbuckling boots
for a first edition of Edward Lear's poetry
and sails away at the end of summer
from the light switches of the neighbourhood
into the darkness beyond Millbay Docks.

The Old Wooden Bridge

In summer I fish for nothing
off the edge of the old wooden bridge
the past sits to the right
the future on the left
three pairs of feet dangling into space.

Bobbie Gentry's *Ode to Billie Joe*
I sing to myself and the river adds
a bit of Handel to the mix.

On the old wooden bridge
on the bus into town
I read stories by Kahlil Gibran
and Mullah Nasruddin.
Elsewhere I read
Lewis Carroll to the rabbits
and Bashō to the frogs.
This is my home
my haven from the big city
and the babble of voices.
My home where I spend
idyllic weekends by the river
rolling around in Class B laughter
and smoking Franklins Mild.
My home where I watch
moths laying siege to storm lamps
singeing their wings on joss sticks
reincarnating on candles.

All roads lead
from the past to the future
from the suburbs to the epicentre
and Llandegley is as quiet
as Llandegley International Airport.

The air-space
above the old caravan site
is home to magpies and rooks
and migrant birds touching down
from transatlantic flights.

Across the green neighbourhood
animals that always remind me of Westerns
look at me with big eyes, big mouths chewing
cow parsley and grass.

Over the hedge
the road leads to Old Radnor
while the river runs its course joyfully
like a child going home for tea.

Was it here
I read *Born in Tibet*
was it here
I got homesick for my hometown
where I've spent the intervening years
sitting in my father's armchair
writing the minutes
of the river's soothing monologue
into my notebook.

Three Quarters of a Ten Bob Note

On a day of sharing tit-bits of suburban mythology
I tell my tall friends I have seen disbelief in eyes
all colours of the rainbow
and I tell them I have walked the streets
of England's biggest city,
a homeless young man of twenty winters
with a family and a hometown
two hundred and thirty seven miles southwest across the dark

and from those days and nights
half a dozen stories have survived
the slow journey into middle age.
The young policeman on South End Green
who gave me a bag of red and green apples
outside the cafe where the grandmasters
of the Borough of Camden played chess,
moving pieces across the board quick as pinball.

Beneath the golden palaces of suburbia
the Northern Line passes through the ground.
Beneath the ticking of the tube station clock
the past retains an oral presence.

George Orwell
worked in the village
in a second-hand bookshop
in the years between publication
of *Down and Out in Paris and London*
and *Homage to Catalonia*.

Aldous Huxley's brother
who I remember from the programme
about animals, vegetables and minerals
lived somewhere in the neighbourhood.

I saw him on several occasions
a man in his early eighties
walking with a cane
back home from the Heath

and I remember with fondness
the woman who said I looked destitute
who dropped Seven and Six into my hand
while I sat, waiting for Christmas
on the steps of the South End Green fountain

and Joseph Guido Farthing
who I met on the first night of my homelessness
and was glad of the company
who introduced me to a plastic lady
he'd picked up that night
from a shop doorway
on Tottenham Court Road
and we sat there for a while
on the steps of the South End Green fountain
the plastic lady on Joe's knee,
quieter than a ventriloquist dummy
she could speak every language in the world
or none at all.

The lady from Tottenham Court Road
fell asleep in the middle of the conversation
while Joe proposed marriage
to every woman he met that night

and then there was the friend
who lived in blissful sin
with a tall red-headed woman
on Parliament Hill.
One winter afternoon
he gave me a key and shelter to sleep
in a car by the side of the road

and one night I dreamed I had a licence
to drive the car all over the world
and be homeless in Europe,
homeless in Asia, homeless in America
driving from petrol pump to petrol pump
joyriding and picking up hitch-hikers
on the road back to consciousness
and when I awoke in the big city
inside this little refuge on wheels
I thought how nice it would be to receive
an invitation to share breakfast
with one of my neighbours
the luxury of wholemeal toast
and a pot of tea in the garden

and then one day I met a writer
who lived in a house by the railway line
between Hampstead and Gospel Oak
the writer was a friend of the woman
who gave me Seven and Six
one day the writer lost his job in the city
after going to work wearing blue slippers,
black pyjamas and I don't remember
the colour of the dressing gown,
but I do remember
spending most of that winter
commuting from my luxury apartment
on Parliament Hill to the Roundhouse
on Chalk Farm Road

and I had a little notebook in those days
in which I filled those days
with longing for a room
in which to write
and now I have that room,
but not a dressing gown
or Seven and Six in old money

and quite recently and quite by chance
I have discovered and fallen in love
with the poetry of Rosemary Tonks
the writer who under the influence of French Surrealism
left the world two slim volumes of poetry.

Rosemary Tonks
was last seen walking in Hampstead
with a mid-life crisis and a liminal ticket
leaving her home on Downshire Hill
she vanished from affluent society,
but left no known photograph
of the vivacious blonde
she was supposed to have been.

The woman in a blue dress
who gave me three quarters of a ten bob note
out of kindness,
out of the night from nowhere
was blonde and vivacious,
but never said whether she wrote poetry
or socialised with the ghost of Baudelaire

and forty years after Rosemary Tonks
left her house keys and fingerprints behind
I wonder now and then what it would be like
to live and sleep in a car
by the side of the road
and be down and out all over the world
begging for pots of tea and wholemeal toast
and Seven and Six at the age of sixty.

The Past

The past pops up like a pop song on a fat jukebox
it snuggles up to the present to keep warm.
Part of the time it's sentimental
like the afterglow of an old movie
crying on the shoulder of Marlene Dietrich.

It's a childhood scrapbook of reminiscences
a game of hide and seek or snakes and ladders
a motorbike and sidecar on Montacute Avenue
a road sign reading Memory Lane closed for repairs
a traffic light on red or green or preserved in amber
a fingerprint of innocence left behind.

It could be the footpath
my dad carried home from Shakey Bridge
and left leaning against the fireplace
which kept us warm through a cold
and wild West Park winter

or Miss Paris ticking her way
through the years on Little Dock Lane
teaching us how to spell Honicknowle
getting gold stars to hang in the night sky
above sketches of Woodland Fort
silver and bronze for homework
and nothing out of ten for custard.

The past is dark,
but there's light at the end of the lamp post
it's an old friend a gift to the present
a long season I stretch for on tiptoe
to touch the ceiling of the day before.

It's a wardrobe of wedding dresses
in a suburban guest house
I pass through this museum of matrimony
on a honeymoon back to the big day,
singing Junior Walker and Jason Isbell.

The past has a future
in the Drake Circus branch of Waterstone's
forty three poems from the Honicknowle Hills
have been muscled out
by yet another Keats retrospective.

The past is a glove waving from a fence post
a neighbourhood of prefabs and plimsolls
a shadow in the form of a small boy
hanging around in the school playground
on the street corner, running through the park.
I can still hear that small boy's echo
resonate in my voice.

Seven Years in Honicknowle

When I was small my mother would bounce me
up and down on her Buddhist knee and tell stories
about the Dalai Lama, the yeti and Lobsang Rampa.

I thought the yeti was a Himalayan mountain man
who climbed Mount Everest like Edmund Hillary
and stuck a flag of Tibet on the roof of the world
as snow fell from the sky and landed on the flag
of New Zealand.

The yeti had some cousins who came from Dorset
who sang Tibetan folk songs and had beards as long
as straw

When the Yetis toured Tibet
they sang Christmas carols on Christmas Eve
on the Dalai Lama's doorstep
and headlined in the night clubs of Lhasa
which may not quite be Glastonbury
the Fillmore East or rock and roll,
but then neither is *Yakety Yak*.

My mother spent seven years down on Farm Lane
at the Honicknowle Labour Club pulling pints
and left-wingers.

She believes in reincarnation
and thinks it's about time
the Yetis made a comeback
playing in venues packed
with yak herders again.

She was born at sea level
like the mermaids and me

then moved up the river to Little Tibet
where she went to primary school
with Lobsang Rampa.
When I first read Lobsang Rampa
I wondered if my third eye
was brown or blue.

The Van Dike Club

From the prefabs
on Tamar Way
to the Van Dike Club
on Exmouth Road
where I saw Led Zeppelin
before they became Norse gods.
In this small club
perched above the railway line
that runs from Shakey Bridge to town
I saw John Paul Jones, John Bonham,
Robert Plant and Jimmy Page.

I was seventeen years old.
Six months out
of Honicknowle Secondary.
I was six foot two,
wearing Cuban heels
and a shit-brown suit.
That night I caught the bus
into town and bumped into
a trio of old school friends
midway between the Barley Sheaf
and Pete Russell's Hot Record Store
on the corner of Market Avenue.

A couple of beers under
our Wild West Park belts
we boarded the bus
to the Van Dike Club
for a night of rock and roll
while behind us the juke box
belted out hits from the pop charts.

On the way out to Exmouth Road
I stared into the future of the night
where I saw my friends hugging the bar
while I stood alone
tapping my left foot
on the edge of the dance floor.
I was within walking distance
of Robert Plant.

I was a teenager in exile
from *Two Way Family Favourites*.
a stranger in a polyester shirt
the night I chucked Bing Crosby
for rock and roll.
Overdressed
and conspicuous like a mod
on the streets of Modbury
I returned the next weekend
in jeans and ripped jumper
mixing with working class
and middle class kids from Mannamead
and the People's Republic of Whitleigh.

Hanging out in The Van Dike
I saw the Third Ear Band,
but not the Camels Head Bangers
the Eurovision Snog Contest
Donald's Metaphysical Greenhouse
Safe As Toast or Punk Yoga.

One night I scored a quid deal
wrapped in silver paper
and got stoned
with Steve and Adrian
in old railway tunnels
under Kings Road.
The tunnels were an ideal

rehearsal space
for an underground band
so we strapped on our guitars
and started jamming
with Dead Rock Stars
in the Afterlife
and the Sons and Daughters
of the Baby Boom.
Back at Exmouth Road
I fell asleep in the cloakroom,
got kicked out by Pete Van Dike
and spent the rest of the evening
tapping my left foot to King Crimson
throwing up to the twang
of *Twenty First Century Schizoid Man*
on the edge of Devonport Park.

Smoked more pot
with Derek the Disc Jockey
Milky Bar Kid lookalike
and other chocolate-themed friends
the night Fairport Convention played
and two coachloads of police raided
and found nothing but dust in my pockets.
The Van Dike was hot
and crowded that night
so I moved outside to get some air.
Some twenty folk-rock minutes later
when the police cruised
down Exmouth Road
the Dansette in my head
was playing Sandy Denny
singing Richard Thompson's

Meet on the Ledge
from Fairport's
What We Did on Our Holidays.

When I saw uniforms
moving towards the Van Dike
through the dodgy lenses
of my stoned haze
I thought it was a bunch
of brass band players
on a Salvation Army outing.
That night we had great fun
taunting the massed band
of the Old Bill as they moved
us slowly down the street
towards the Devonport Road.

In the aftermath
the police were slated
in the media for sending
teenagers home in the cold
without hats and coats
which were left hanging overnight
in the psychedelic quiet
of the Van Dike's cloakroom.

One night
I was reading poetry there
probably the Cow Poem
when someone dropped
a glockenspiel on stage
a subtle counterpoint.
This was the night Frank Charm
dressed as Father Christmas
handed out joints
to all the badly behaved children.

At the Van Dike I saw Family
and Free and an American band
called Daddy Longlegs.
I saw Keith Emerson of the Nice

stick knives into his keyboards,
distorting Leonard Bernstein
and *America*.
I saw Adrian Henri's band
the Liverpool Scene.
Ten shillings to get in the door
and take a ride
on *A Tramcar to Frankenstein*.
The night after I missed
the Bonzo Dog Doo-Dah Band
a crew of urban spacemen
waved to me while driving
through Stoke Village
the following morning.

Shortly after Led Zeppelin and I
had made our debuts at the Van Dike
I bumped into a blues harp player
by the zebra crossing outside Dingles.
The harp player who'd jammed
with Champion Jack Dupree
introduced me to the works
of Aldous Huxley and J.R.R. Tolkien.
The harp player blew smoke rings
and talked about smoking grass
in Anns Place.
At first I thought Ann was a friend of his,
but she turned out to be the name of a street.

In Anns Place
I met Albert Fischer
better known as the Bishop.
The night I met Albert he read extracts
from Alfred Noyes' *The Highwayman*
while drunk on rough cider.

Around this time I rode the bus
from Honicknowle to Exmouth Road
humming Steve Miller's *Quicksilver Girl*
and Melanie's *Bo Bo's Party*.
I had a pocket full of joss sticks
and a season ticket
for the Aquarian Age.
I was rocking and rolling up
on Exmouth Road.
I was forty years away
from becoming a household name
like Pink Floyd and fish fingers.

Some nights
I'd catch the last bus home
to watch *Monty Python's Flying Circus*.
Laughing my socks off while my mum
sat across the sofa from me and frowned.
My mum was keen on Val Doonican
and Jimmy Tarbuck while my dad liked
Sandie Shaw and bagpipe music
and read Robert Louis Stevenson
and James Fenimore Cooper.

I read the *Desiderata*,
The Narrow Road to the Deep North
and Other Travel Sketches and
By Grand Central Station
I Sat Down and Wept.

I was the only member of my family
who ever went to the Van Dike
and later the Roundhouse and Ronnie's.

The weekend Jethro Tull appeared
they played virtually everything
from *This Was*.

Up on the Van Dike's small stage
Mick Abrahams, Clive Bunker, Glenn Cornick
and Ian Anderson standing on one leg
left foot balanced above the right knee
playing the pirate, playing the flute
a little bit of showmanship
for the council estate crowd
which was almost as good
as that *Top of the Pops* clip
of Bill Wyman's bass
sticking up in the air
like a big finger.

That night while the fanfare
in my head played Copland
The Buckingham Shed Collective
drove up to the club in a Ford Zodiac.
Falling under the influence
of rock and roll after a long day
potato picking in the South Hams.

When The Buckingham Shed Collective
walked down Exmouth Road
they looked more like tractor drivers
than rock stars.
When they walked into the Van Dike
I was standing on the steps
above the dance floor
tapping my left foot
as Anderson's flute paid homage
to Roland Kirk's *Serenade to a Cuckoo*.

I was a teenager with a bad haircut
when I first went to the Van Dike Club.
After I saw Led Zeppelin
I grew my hair down to my shoulders,
but it didn't improve my guitar playing

so I switched to drums and progressed
from there to progressive rock
to tripping across the landscapes of town
turning up rolling a joint and zonking out
to Canned Heat, Country Joe and the Fish
and Creedence Clearwater Revival.
Playing acid rock on psychedelic Dansettes
tapping my left foot to the Grateful Dead,
Quicksilver Messenger Service
and Big Brother and the Holding Company
or stopping off at Jack's Joint
at the bottom of Albert Road
for one last cup of coffee
before heading down to Shakey Bridge
a caravan of teenagers
passing through Camels Head
edging closer to Abercrombie Lane
and another wild weekend
on the sofas of the housing estate
with Marianne and Nancy.

A Long Weekend on the Sofa

The aisles are quiet today
no-one is opening anything
not even a door.
I'm wondering whether
it was like this
for Hemingway and Miller
when they first arrived
from woodwork class.

I'm squashed on the second floor
between Kipling and O'Hara
can you come and pick me up
and take me down to the table
by the big bay window
open me on page thirty seven
and you'll be hooked.
I'm waiting and while
I'm in the process
I notice the clock
handcuffed to the wall
it's got three hands
which is one more
than Lobsang Rampa.

Is it the weekend
or the start of another holiday?
I could do with some time off
A day trip to some beauty spot.
Maybe run off with an encyclopaedia
of modern art.

Did Hemingway and Miller
ever come here and socialise
with their books.

Did you know when I was young
I used to think William Somerset Maugham
was born in Somerset, but he wasn't
he was born in Paris and died in Nice
the year before England won the World Cup.
When Geoff Hurst hit number four
shortly after Somerset's death
there was dancing and singing
in the streets of Wincanton
and Weston-Super-Mare.

Did you know Shakespeare Road
has had more influence on me
than Byron Avenue and Tennyson Gardens
and did you know there's hundreds
of languages spoken in the world
and I haven't had a good natter in years
or nodded off to some bedtime story.
My favourites are *Heidi* and *Huckleberry Finn*.

Ever since I've been here
I feel like an old man in a residential home
who no-one comes to visit.

Can I come to your house for Christmas
do you live in a cowboy town
like El Paso or Laredo
can we go on a cattle drive
to Dodge City or Abilene
spend New Year in New Mexico
either Santa Fe or Albuquerque.

Zane Grey wants to drive
down to Durango at sundown
Ned Buntline's gone back
to the bright lights of Tombstone
back to where the Wild West

is a bat-swing door
away from peace and quiet.
It's so quiet around here
you could hear
a Penny Dreadful drop.

The last time James Fennimore Cooper
left the library he took an overnight train
to Wichita in Eighteen Fifty Seven.

Larry McMurtry's hanging out
with Cormac McCarthy in Texas
Walt Whitman's in North Dakota
on the Deadwood stage
stuck in a traffic jam.

I'm stuck with Rudyard and Frank
pretending you're Santa Claus
to a screenwriter whose going to turn
The Honicknowle Book of the Dead
into the next spaghetti western.
On the soundtrack
I imagine Leonard Cohen
singing *Born to be Wild*
and Lobsang Rampa
twirling the microphone
for The Honicknowle Blues Band
on *Two Out of Three Ain't Bad*
and *Three Wheels on my Wagon.*

If Pearl and Dean open
for The Honicknowle Blues Band
in the Belgrave or the Ford Palladium
it may put Hollywood on the A to Z.

In a voice borrowed
from old pirate films

shown on television screens
in the prefabs of Wild West Park
and Little America
I'd like to hear the Dalai Lama
and Geraldine Monk reading
The Honicknowle Book of the Dead
in Tibetan and English
while I spend
a long weekend on the sofa
with Jules Verne and Agatha Christie.

Sunset in some small town
would be a welcome distraction
from this vigil with Rudyard Kipling
and Frank O'Hara.

Maybe we could sit around the Dansette
next Halloween and listen to Led Zeppelin
then crank up the volume for the Drive-By Truckers

Maybe you like wild parties
we could do with one around here
for a week or two.

Playing Chess in Chatsworth Gardens

Playing chess
with Peter Allen

Chatsworth Gardens
to Sherford Crescent

Kedlestone Avenue
to Woolaton Grove

Honicknowle Secondary
to West Park Infants

black and white
like television.

Kings and queens
topple into and out of bed

in three bedroom
palaces on Princess Avenue

bishops in the churchyard
and wardrobe mistresses

in the Blue Monkey
flirt through the door

head for barn dances
in Barne Barton

and Tupperware parties
in Weston Mill.

Rooks in Woodland Wood
discuss tautology

pawns in the pawn shop
sing Bob Dylan.

I stare through
the dining room window

across the park of possibility
see knights in lumberjack shirts

walking corgis home
to Buckingham Shed

to watch repeats
of Royal Weddings.

Playing chess
with Peter Allen

Shakey Bridge
to Sidmouth Junction

State Hill
to Broomball Lane.

Black and white
like a zebra crossing

Penguin Modern Poets
Times New Roman.

A Supermarket in Honicknowle

What thoughts I have of you tonight, Walt Whitman
— Allen Ginsberg, *A Supermarket in California*

So where are you tonight
Allen Ginsberg
now that the supermarket has closed
and Santa Claus has gone back home
to wrap up warmly for Christmas
and the checkout girl from California
has flown across the Atlantic
to spend New Year in America
with the store detective
from your imagination.

Are you on the same flight
reading *Sunflower Sutra*
or out in the car park with Jack
waiting for a train
that passes through
the Nineteen Fifties
or are you pushing
shopping trolleys across the night
to distant high streets of the heart.

Are you working in a supermarket
or selling sunflowers
at the end of a switchboard line
chanting Buddhist mantras
over the tannoy
to get yourself through
another supermarket day
your voice moving
from department to department
calling workers on the shop floor,
workers in short-sleeved shirts

dressing shelves
and serving images to customers
or are you working the night shift
trying to make ends meet
like two old friends on a street corner.

So where are you tonight
Allen Ginsberg
are you haunting the dreams
of the next generation of writers
reading poetry
in dream supermarkets of the night
as you cruise the aisles
shopping for inspiration
filling your shopping trolley
with sunflower oil
and Valentine cards
for everyone you've ever loved.

And where are they now
where are all of my old
teenage friends from childhood
those cowboys from the corner shop.
I've not seen any of them for generations.
Are they happily married to television
or out walking the streets,
homeless shadows looking for shelter
and strangers to love.
Have they been consumed
by the Consumer Society
recycling themselves like Himalayan monks
or egg boxes in the cardboard bailer.
Have they fallen
into the black hole of capitalism
like Harpers garage
and Pete Russell's Hot Record Store.

I'm working in a supermarket now
serving lunch to Mrs. Flatfish,
The Witch and the Wardrobe
and the Five to Five Man
working with my grand-daughter
reading *Guthrie to Ginsberg*
and other poems in church halls
and libraries
all the way from the Honicknowle Hills
to the outskirts of town,
but I've never read
in a supermarket in California
or in the dining room of the Beat Hotel.

I remember the night you shared the stage
with Peter Orlovsky at the Lower Guildhall
on the corner of Catherine Street
and I remember that night
wanting to hear the lonesome whistle
of a locomotive replace the car horns
and scooters on Royal Parade
remember wanting to hear you read
Howl and *Sunflower Sutra*
for the Buddhists and the beatniks,
the prehistoric penguins
and the train spotters
wearing halos of nostalgia
and long hair in the crowd,
but you didn't read
any of that old City Lights stuff
or bring Gregory Corso,
Lawrence Ferlinghetti
or the store detective from California
out from behind the curtains
to make their debuts
at the Lower Guildhall,
no trio of Penguin Modern Poets

no bunches of sunflowers
no shoplifters in the crowd
crossing the car park
with books of poetry.

That night at the Lower Guildhall
as we passed through evening stardust
you drew a sunflower
two or three inches tall
a black sunflower from America
which took root like a memory
and found a home
on the windowsill of my room
overlooking the park
and one afternoon
as March gave way to April
I found a packet of sunflower seeds
in a corner of old shadows
in my father's garden shed
which I planted
to brighten the neighbourhood
a galaxy of sunflowers
constellations of them
all over the slopes
of Honicknowle and West Park.

The sunflower you drew is thirty years old now
thirty years since I stood in front of the stage
with Allen Clarke and Bernard Brotherton
and smoked cigarettes with Peter Orlovsky
until he realised it wasn't weed.

Tim Allen was there
unknown to me then
one of two hundred strangers
in the beat poetry crowd,
but I didn't see the store detective

was he hiding backstage
or lingering by the bookstall
did he follow you
periodically through the years
until his shadow grew thin.

Before I read you I knew nothing
about supermarkets or sunflowers
knew nothing about Lorca,
Whitman or Kerouac.
By the time I'd negotiated
the foothills of adolescence
I'd read snatches of T.S. Eliot,
Alfred Noyes and Ogden Nash
and listened to the blues singer,
Bessie Smith
in Kenny Frost's house
on Shakespeare Road
when I was fifteen and still at school
and now I'm approaching sixty
and my shadow is pointed
towards the supermarket
and the moon is following me
across the still forms
of sleeping policemen in the road

and you where are you tonight
Allen Ginsberg
are you walking home
with all those other beat poets of the night
while I'm walking around in crazy circles
outside a supermarket in Honicknowle
under the constellation of the sunflower
from where Walt Whitman sends his regards.

The Old Writing Desk

I'm in love with an old writing desk
that lives a couple of miles across town
on the wrong side of the Hyde Park Road
antique shop window.

Every time I'm in this part of Peverell
I check to see if the writing desk
has been absorbed
back into the ether
of middle class suburbia.

The price
somewhere
in the snowy altitudes
of two thousand quid
is a bit too far above sea level
for my share of the laundry.

I hate the thought of the writing desk
spending time in the home of a crime novelist
or belonging to a writer of short stories
or becoming the private property
of some captain of monologues.

Sid Pluto tells me
you can pick up a quality writing desk
at the local auction rooms
and still have enough money left over
for a year of decadent and domestic affairs,
but would there be another writing desk
quite as feminine as this goddess of wood.

If I had the money
I would take the writing desk

home to my house
on the edge of the St. Budeaux Triangle
and introduce it to all my other pieces
of furniture.

Maybe today or maybe tomorrow
I'll get lucky with a lucky dip
or inherit the housing estate
or the offshore banking account
of a church mouse
and maybe the day after that
I'll pay off the mortgage
and plonk a wad of cash
down on the counter
and save the writing desk
the heartache of another
lonely night in Peverell.

The Newspaper Round

The newspaper round begins
with the *Morning Star*
and Venus in a bright yellow dress
infertile in a bath of sulphuric rapture.
At six I fall out of bed
like no angel ever did
and land at the breakfast table.
There are no prayers in this house
to give thanks to toast or cereal
though as I lay
my newspaper boy feet
on the dining room floor
I would like to thank the Earth
which gives us vegetables
and a home in the shadows
of the astral.

No God cycles my father
to the church at St. Levan
no goddess
helps my mother bake saffron
or hang washing
or writes poems or homework
my own work on the sideboard.
I jot nightmares
and the doggerel of adolescence
is the poet in residence
inside my pen top
it's like a miniature
Milky Way inside
a galaxy of gold stars
stuck here and there
on a tree's old skin.

Full of breakfast
and news of the Great Train Robbery
I hum the theme tune to *Ivor the Engine*
push my bicycle across the main road
and lean it against the wall of Easterbrooks.
I walk in with West Park in my eyes
and out with Fleet Street on my shoulder.

The rain falling
on my newspaper round
looks sad on my plimsolls.

Houses I walk up to like a stranger
shine a warm light of cheer
I want to be in that land
on the other side of the window
I want to sit in a deckchair
in the holiday resort of room temperature
I'm shivering and the sun has been delayed
somewhere east of Peverell.
The sun is old
older than my dad
it reads the newspaper
and hides behind it
the newspaper catches fire
and the fire engines are called
and the paparazzi come
to their own cremation.

The newspaper round begins
the newspaper round
is not quite circular
like a poetry circle
or the gate wheel at Woodland Fort
or the garden pond on Marratt Road
where Lobsang Rampa's aunty lives.

The newspaper round begins
with a stick of chewing gum
and a packet of Wagon Wheels
it starts with a bedtime story
and ends with a Queen Log
kiss and tell in Woodland Wood.

I walk in circles in the dark
make ripples in rain puddles
wear a mask depicting Big Ben
and make up the news
as I cycle around.
I award myself
an honorary degree in witchcraft
and a licence to wave
a magic wand in public
and banish all bad news to landfill
and not recycle it
to celebrate I suck Spangles
and Gobstoppers
and sing love songs to Kathy Kirby.

On my newspaper round
I carry a torch inside my newspaper bag
to shine in the eyes of news-flashes
who hang around in press gangs
and cycle up and down
the street in the dark
competing with each other for publicity.

The newspaper round begins
between the cat flap and the letterbox
the newspaper stretches out
passive in the throes of history
across the epicentre of the coffee table.

Newspapers wear black and white skirts
cut down to size from the long legs of trees
dogs with a grip on current affairs
rise up from doormats.

The newspaper round repeats itself
like history and my dad
thirteen times a week
Fleet Street follows Fleet Street
through the door of Easterbrooks
and down the Crownhill Road.

Leaning from left to right
I walk under the umbrella of history
with my head in the news
the tabloids I launch through letterboxes
like big paper aeroplanes
are as slim as Jean Shrimpton.

A Short History of the Past

Tonight I sit in a circle
of old photographs
and old friends,
peer back down the tunnel
from thirty seven years
into the future
as the past creeps in
and attaches itself like a cat
throws a stick
for the dog of memory
to chase across the years
back to the rustic heart
of Nineteen Seventy Four
to the old caravan site
beneath Llandegley Rocks
to a time before
Llandegley International Airport
and terminals one and three
were born
before volcanic dust
followed the recession from Iceland
grounded assets and air-travel
and left luggage all over the world.

Somewhere on the outskirts of memory
I catch a glimpse of my younger self
and see the young faces of my old friends
sons and daughters of the baby boom
riding the Saturday afternoon bus
to Pritchard's garage in Llandrindod Wells.

Passing through Penybont we break into a medley
of *Marrakesh Express*, *Sunny Afternoon*
and *Born to Be Wild*

and between one paper bag and the next
the bus shape-shifts into a Tennessee Williams cat
screeching through Crossgates on the way into town.
Forty miles an hour, racing the train, racing the river
the shopping trip bus stops in a dead heat
with the reflection of itself in the garage window.

Tonight here in the dining room of a shed
on the slopes of the Honicknowle Hills
I sit in my father's armchair
and write a short history of the past
following the road map that got me here
I follow my footsteps back
to the small town heart of Saturday afternoon
go searching for the nostalgia of daily life
go shuffling along Middleton Street
in a worn pair of desert boots
passing over fleeting portraits of old friends
in galleries of rain puddles filling the ground.

Under the rooftop of another day
I skip across the years and pavement cracks
play leapfrog over the old railway bridge
become invisible like the smoke ring ghost
of a cigarette smoker
in the smoke of a passing train
dancing down the hill
to chew a slice of old cow pie
to meet the memory of myself for lunch
a Rosicrucian fry-up and apple crumble
in the La Roma Cafe.

On the slopes below Five Ways
I reacquaint myself with the jukebox
which plays Bachman Turner Overdrive
over plates of eggs, beans and chips
and Doctor Who's favourite band
over games of pinball.

After lunch I roll cigarettes
and blow smoke rings
like the twenty a day magician
in Tolkien's trilogy,
my bright blue eyes twinkling
in a fog of Franklin's Mild.

Outside the rain has eased
to a library-like whisper.

Under the influence of Jesse James
I climb the hill to the bookshop.
Under the influence of black coffee
I think about love and peace and gunfights
think how the pen kills as casually
as the sun going down in a western.

Under the constellation of science fiction
I pay twenty five pieces of stardust
for Robert Silverberg.

Under my red jumper
the shopping list in my shirt pocket
is a map of the town.

Grunge

after Jenny Joseph

When I grow old
which can't be any more
than a couple of weeks away
I promise not to wear
a knotted handkerchief on my head
or purple reading glasses in public.

If my sense of colour
should slip into the red
and you see me wearing orange shoes,
an old school tie, a pink top hat
and advocating the virtues of voting Tory
then please stick my head under the shower
and rinse the dye from my hair.

If in the spirit of compromise
you donate your hot pants
and platform shoes to Oxfam
I'll dig out my gold medallions
and tracksuit bottoms
and run them down to Cancer Research.

If you acknowledge the satirical elegance
of my green flairs and turtleneck sweaters
I'll return the compliment
when you step out of the stretch limousine
in Doc Martens and dungarees,
air-microphone in your hand
miming to a song by the Indigo Girls.

When I grow old
I'll take you out on a date
and we'll walk

hand in hand in the rain
along Old Town Street
two Valentine cards from another age
you all safety pins, Sex Pistols and the Clash
me fifty per cent of Maurice Chevalier
and Hermione Gingold.

When my bus pass arrives
which can't be anymore
than a couple of light years away
I'll travel with a spray can
all over the hills of childhood
and paint the town Picasso.

When I grow old
as old as the old man of my genes.

Buckingham Shed

Some children have imaginary friends.
I had a shed, a gate and a map
which led to an unexplored garden
a polo stroke away
from a big overgrown house.
If I peeked through
the shed's weathered boards
I could turn this big house
into a big palace
turn the east wing into an aviary
the west wing
into a museum of scarecrows
fly flags of robins in the parks
and the fields of the countryside
which I'd pass through
until my pocket money ran out
and I'd be back in my shed
growing magically-modified turnips
and thinking about the train
leaving platform eleven
from my imaginary railway station in life.

I carried my garden shed to school
and out on my newspaper round.
I smuggled it
on the bus to town
and smuggled it back.
I took it to see
Lady Chatterley's Lover at the Gaumont
and stood with it at the end
when they played the National Anthem.

Back in Wild West Park
I took it out

with my imaginary pack of feral cats
and hunted imaginary corgis.
I was born in November
two days after Halloween.
The day I started secondary school
my mother sent me the keys
to Buckingham Shed
and a kingdom of weeds
while my father gave me
an exercise book
and a Mickey Mouse pen
with which I wrote Christmas speeches
from the monarchy in the shadows.

When I was small
I'd sing pop songs all over utopia
and I'd be rich and famous
and meet Alan Freeman,
David Jacobs and Cathy McGowan.

My first rock and roll band
were called The Buckingham Shed Collective.
They were always top of the bill
and talk of the allotment.

In Buckingham Shed
I was taller than any tree
I ever climbed in Woodland Wood.

In my shed I'd flick through
wildlife shots of wise old owls
and read *Trout Fishing on Treasure Island*
as they filled their larders with field mice.
Sometimes the owls would discuss
critical theory with a flock of crows
under an imaginary sky
under which Ted Hughes was standing

the last in a long line
of collected Poet Laureates
each one wearing a poetry medal
for services to the imagination.

The Blue Monkey

In the village of Higher St. Budeaux
all that remains of the Blue Monkey
is a nostalgic finger
a totem pole
for the ghosts of drunken revellers
to dance around and quietly fall over
legless in the dirt.

On the Crownhill Road
I dive off the kerb of the future
into the gutter of the past,
but sense no sense of Guy Fawkes
lingering in the shadows of the church.

On the road south of Weston Mill cemetery
the Camels Head fire crew come screeching
like a bat out of Shakey bridge
too late to save the Blue Monkey
from being gutted
and scattered to the four winds
of archaeology
like a Viking longboat burning to ash.

Headlights out on the Parkway
head for post-war housing estates
and the suburbs of distant towns.
A funeral procession
on the slopes of the valley
driving back through brightness.

On the corner of Dunstone Avenue
children converge like moths
drawn by the grapevine
of smoke and voices.

At the sunset end of the Crownhill Road
nothing moves in the graveyard
no ripple from the other side of the river
no huddle of grief or curiosity
no rain falls through the fingers of night
or phoenix rises after crash-landing
in Higher St. Budeaux
nothing here but the wind and the smoke
and the memory of dancing and singing
in the Blue Monkey.

Crossing the top of Marrett Road
I walk through the ghost town
of my youth and childhood
cough and wipe the past from my eyes
lean briefly against the shoulders
of inebriated friends and strangers
see the bright lights
of weekends and weddings
twinkling in the windows of another time.
As the old blue simian burns
I pray for rain puddles
and make my way home
to a house on the edge of the park.

Some Imaginary Bands

A Plague of Psychedelic Lollypop Ladies

Bashō and the Bash Street Kids

Dead Rock Stars In The Afterlife

Donald's Metaphysical Greenhouse

Drop Dead Ugly

Forty Six Faces of Alice

Heather Grunge

Marshmellow Milton

Paradox Lost

Punk Yoga

Sid Pluto

Sons and Daughters of the Baby Boom

Talk of the Town Hall Groupies

The Eurovision Snog Contest

The Tibetan Roofing Company

Featherweight

My boxing career was short-lived.
I was stopped in the first round.
I can't remember whether
I was in the blue or the red corner
and whether Cassius Clay
was there at the ringside
floating like a heavyweight
and stinging like a B. B. King guitar solo.

I wanted to box for Honicknowle
and be the talk of the housing estate
and the village so I trained hard
shadow boxing in the box-room
punching the lights
out of the National Grid.

I wanted to be a featherweight
like a robin leaning on a garden fork.
I wanted the fight to be broadcast
by the BBC and the commentator
to be Miss Applegate.

I wanted to return in triumph
on a Triumph Bonneville to Buckingham Shed
and be given the keys to Woodland Fort
and the freedom of the West Park chippie.

I wanted my fifteen minutes
of Andy Warhol
in the school playground.

I didn't want to be carried
out of the ring on a stretcher
and paraded through the streets

of Crownhill like something
out of *Emergency Ward Ten.*

I was on the way down
to the canvas of Mount Lonsdale
when the sport teacher
threw in the towel.

I wanted my name to be read out
by Mister Sparrow in school assembly,
but when he didn't mention
my record breaking defeat
in fifty-nine seconds
I wasn't sure
whether to feel relieved
or insulted by his failure.
My only regret
is that I never made it
to Madison Square Gardens
to slug it out with Paul Simon.

Hometown

My hometown is the hometown
of The Camels Head Bangers,
A Plague of Psychedelic Lollypop Ladies
and The Eurovision Snog Contest.

It's the hometown
of Westward Television
where the ghost of Gus Honeybun
still jumps up and down
and sends birthday greetings
to the children of the city.

My hometown is the hometown
of Herchel Smith, Richard Greene,
Punk Yoga, Pennycross Stadium,
the Blue Monkey, Woodland Wood
and The Forty Six Faces of Alice.

It's the hometown of the Van Dike Club
Pete Russell's Hot Record Store
Guy Burgess and Sid Pluto

It's the hometown
of Ron Goodwin
and the Bus Station Loonies
the Honicknowle Blues Band
and The Buckingham Shed Collective

and a lot of other people
who went down
the Mayflower Steps
and never came back.

Notes

PLYMOUTH STREETS MENTIONED IN THE BOOK

Box Hill (local name for Honicknowle Lane)

Broomball Lane	Chatsworth Gardens
Cobbitt Road	Compton Avenue
Coombe Park Lane	Crownhill Road
Devonport Road	Dickens Road
Drake Circus	Exmouth Road
Hirmandale Road	Hyde Park Road
Kedlestone Avenue	Marratt Road
Market Avenue	Montacute Avenue
North Hill	Old Town Street
Paradise Road	Royal Parade
Sherford Crescent	State Hill
Tamar Way	Tennyson Gardens
Woolaton Grove	

PLYMOUTH DISTRICTS MENTIONED IN THE BOOK

Badgers Wood	Camels Head	Crownhill
Efford	Ford Park	Manadon
Mannamead	Holly Park	Honicknowle
Laira	Millbay	Mount Wise
Mutley Plain	Peverell	St Budeaux
Tamerton Foliot	Thorn Park	West Park
Weston Mill	Whitleigh	

OTHER PLACES OF NOTE IN PLYMOUTH

Dingles – Plymouth's premier department store.

Derry's Clock – one of the few pre-war landmarks in the city centre to survive the wartime bombing. Situated at the western end of Royal Parade.

Drake's Island – island in Plymouth Sound.

Mayflower Steps – supposedly the point at which the Pilgrim Fathers set sail from Plymouth for the New World in 1620. They had of course started at Boston, Lincolnshire, and picked up more passengers in the Netherlands and at Southampton; Plymouth was the last port of call before heading across the Atlantic and landing at what is now Plymouth, Massachusetts.

Plym – river on the east side of the city.

Plymouth Sound – the sea off the city; ships anchoring there are protected by the surrounding headlands.

Tamar – river on the west side of the city which acts as the boundary with Cornwall.

Smeaton's Tower – a decommissioned lighthouse, the third to be built (1759)at its original site on the Eddystone Rocks (in the English Channel, 12 miles SSW of Plymouth Sound). After being replaced in 1882, the tower was dismantled and transported to Plymouth Hoe, a promontory above the Sound, where it was opened as a museum in 1884. It remains one of the city's signature landmarks.

Tinside Pool – Lido on the Plymouth waterfront (see cover).

Van Dike Club – Plymouth music venue in the late 1960s and early '70s, at which most of the period's rising rock acts played. The publisher of this volume was obviously at a number of the same gigs as the author, although neither knew it at the time.

Whitsand Bay – beach area near Plymouth.

Woodland Fort – Palmerston fort [q.v.], in Honicknowle.

GLOSSARY OF NAMES AND PLACES

Mick Abrahams (1943–), original guitarist with Jethro Tull; later with Blodwyn Pig.

Ian Anderson (1947–), singer, flautist and guitarist with Jethro Tull.

Louis Aragon (1897-1982), French poet, novelist and WW2 resistance fighter.

Tim Allen, Plymouth poet, now resident in Lancashire.

Pam Ayres (1947–), British poet.

Bashō (1644-1694), Japanese poet.

Elisabeth Bletsoe, British poet.

Bonzo Dog Doo-Dah Band : British novelty rock band (active 1962-1970, but there were later reincarnations).

Born in Tibet – book by Chögyam Trumpa, first published in 1966.

Born to be Wild – hit song by Steppenwolf [q.v.] (1968).

By Grand Central Station…, published 1945, is a novel / prose-poem collection by the Canadian writer Elizabeth Smart (1913-1986), former wife of the English poet, George Barker (1913-1991).

Clive Bunker (1946–), Jethro Tull's original drummer.

Guy Burgess (1911-1963), notorious double agent who was recruited by the KGB while still at Cambridge. He later worked for MI6 and subsequently defected to the USSR. He was born in Devonport, now part of Plymouth.

Maurice Chevalier (1888-1972), French singer and actor.

Cassius Clay (1942-2016), American boxer, later known as Muhammad Ali.

Kelvin Corcoran (1956–), British poet.

Glenn Cornick (1947-2014), Jethro Tull's original bass-player.

Gregory Corso (1930-2001), American Beat poet (1930-2001).

Daddy Long Legs – American rock band (active in the UK 1969-73).

Dansette – brand of record-player popular in the 1960s.

Sandy Denny (1947-1978), British singer; sang with Fairport Convention and, later, Fotheringay. Also a solo act.

Desiderata is a prose poem by the US writer Max Hermann (1872-1945). Written in 1925, it became popular in the early '70s.

Champion Jack Dupree (1910-1992), American blues pianist and singer active in the UK.

Keith Emerson (1944-2016), British rock musician; keyboard player with The Nice [q.v.] and later, Emerson, Lake and Palmer.

Fairport Convention – British folk-rock band that started out in the 1960s, and is still active after many personnel changes.

Family – British rock band (active 1966-1973).

Lawrence Ferlinghetti (1919–), American beat poet and publisher of City Lights Editions.

Fillmore East – San Francisco music venue in the 1960s and '70s.

Free – British rock band (active 1968-1973).

Roy Fuller (1912-1991), British poet.

Damian Furniss (1966–), British poet.

Gandy Street – in Exeter.

Hermione Gingold (1897-1987), British movie actress.

Bobbie Gentry (1944–), American singer-songwriter famous for 'Ode to Billie Joe' (1967).

Kahlil Gibran (1883-1931), Lebanese-American writer, especially famous for *The Prophet*. A Maronite Christian, his syncretic writings also take in Sufi and Islamic influences.

Ron Goodwin (1925-2003), British film composer, born in Plymouth.

Harry Guest (1930–), British poet.

Woody Guthrie (1912-1967), American folksinger.

John Hall (1945–), British poet.

Lee Harwood (1939-2015), British poet.

Hatherleigh – market town in West Devon.

Adrian Henri (1932-2000), British poet, artist, singer.

Herzog – Werner Herzog (1942–), German film director.

Edmund Hillary (1919-2008), first man to climb Mt. Everest (1952).

Gus Honeybun – puppet rabbit on Westward TV (ITV), Plymouth studios from 1961-1992. His main task was to hop or jump while his accomplice read birthday greetings to watching children.

Lightnin' Hopkins (1912-1982), American blues singer.

Billie Holiday (1915-1959), American jazz singer.

Miroslav Holub (1923-1998), Czech poet.

Geoff Hurst (1941–), English footballer; scorer of three goals in the 1966 World Cup Final.

Thomas Ingoldsby, author of the (fake) *Ingoldsby Legends*, published in the 1840s. Pen-name of Richard Harris Barham.

Jason Isbell (1979–), American singer-songwriter.

John Paul Jones (1946–), British rock musician, session-player and composer. Bass-player in Led Zeppelin.

Norman Jope, Plymouth poet.

B.B. King (1925-2015), American blues singer and guitarist.

(Rahsaan) Roland Kirk (1935-1977), American jazz saxophonist.

Philip Kuhn, British poet.

Liverpool Scene – Adrian Henri's [q.v.] band (1967-1972).

Nils Lofgren (1951–), American rock guitarist.

Cormac McCarthy (1933–), American novelist.

Brownie McGhee (1915-1996), American blues singer.

Larry McMurtry (1936–), American novelist, noted for his Westerns.

George Melly (1926-2007), British jazz singer.

Christopher Middleton (1926-2015), British poet.

Mitch Mitchell (1947-2008), British rock musician; drummer with The Jimi Hendrix Experience.

The Munsters – American TV programme (1964-1966)

The Nice – British rock band (active 1967-1970), led by Keith Emerson [q.v.], later of Emerson Lake and Palmer, which played its inaugural concert in Plymouth.

Pete Russell's Hot Record Store – originally a place to buy jazz records, this Plymouth shop morphed into the go-to place for rock albums in the 1960s and 1970s.

Peter Orlovsky (1933-2010), American beat poet.

Jimmy Page (1944–), guitarist in Led Zeppelin.

Palmerston forts – defensive positions erected around the British coast-line in the early 19th century, often close to major potential military objectives, by order of Lord Palmerston. There are several in Plymouth, Woodland Fort being one.

Jaco Pastorius (1951-1987), American jazz bassist.

Penybont (also Pen-y-bont) – a village in Powys, Wales.

Robert Plant (1948–), British rock singer; singer with Led Zeppelin.

Iggy Pop (1947–), American rock singer.

King Crimson – British rock band, still active. '21st Century Schizoid Man' is from their first album *The Court of the Crimson King* (1969).

Llandegley Rocks – NE extremity of a ridge running from Llandrindod Wells.

Llandegley International Airport – spoof location in Radnorshire, Wales: "more than just an airport, and less than just an airport". Road signs exist, but the airport does not. When I stumbled upon Llandegley International Airport – many years after living in Llandegley – it led me to write 'The Old Wooden Bridge' and 'A Short History of the Past'.

Morning Star – newspaper of the Communist Party of Great Britain.

Narrow Road to the Deep North – travel writings and poems by Matsuo Bashō.

Mullah Nasruddin (13th century) – Sufi writer and thinker.

Marrakesh Express – hit song for Crosby, Stills and Nash (1969).

Mary Quant (1934–), British fashion designer who came to prominence in the 1960s.

Lobsang Rampa (pen-name of Cyril Henry Hoskin, 1910-1981), author famous in the 1950s and '60s for his occult writings. He was born in Plympton, now part of Plymouth. A plumber, he claimed to be inhabited by the spirit of a Tibetan lama, who dictated his books. *The Third Eye* was his most famous volume.

Peter Redgrove, British poet (1932-2003).

Jonathan Richman (1951–), American singer-songwriter.

Shangri-Las : '60s American girl-group, famous for 'Leader of the Pack' and 'Remember'.

Sandie Shaw (1947–), British pop singer of the 1960s.

Jean Shrimpton (1942–), British fashion model and actress famous in the 1960s; now a hotelier in Cornwall.

Robert Silverberg (1935–), American SF novelist.

Herchel Smith (1925-2001), organic chemist who made the discoveries that were key to the development of oral and injectable contraceptives. He was born in Plymouth.

Steve Spence, Plymouth poet.

Steppenwolf – '60s American rock band, famous for 'Born to be Wild'.

Jimmy Tarbuck (1940–), British comedian.

Richard Thompson (1949–), British guitarist and song-writer; original guitarist of Fairport Convention.

Rosemary Tonks (1928-2014), British poet of the 1960s who disappeared after joining a strict religious sect, and stopped writing. Her collected poems were brought back into print after her death by Bloodaxe Books.

Sid Vicious (1957-1979), bass player with the Sex Pistols.

Sunny Afternoon – hit song by The Kinks (1966).

Dame Joan Vickers (1907-1994), Conservative MP for Plymouth, Devonport from 1955-1974. Created a Baroness in 1974.

The Voice Thrower is a book by Tim Allen [q.v.].

Junior Walker (1931-1995), R&B / soul singer, and sax-player, who recorded for the Motown label with his band, Junior Walker & the All-Stars.

Wallace Arnold – holiday coach-tour company, now merged into Shearings.

Muddy Waters (1913-1983), American blues singer/guitarist.

What We Did on Our Holidays – 1969 album by Fairport Covention [q.v.].

Big Joe Williams (1903-1982), American blues singer/guitarist.

Woodbury Salterton – Devon village, near Exeter.

Yakety-Yak – rock'n'roll novelty song recorded by The Coasters (1958).

Warren Zevon (1947-2003), American singer-songwriter.

Lightning Source UK Ltd.
Milton Keynes UK
UKOW01f2331211016

285877UK00001B/54/P